Ice-Age Monsters
Megaceros

Written by Rupert Oliver
Illustrated by Andrew Howat

Library of Congress Cataloging in Publication Data

Oliver, Rupert.
  Megaceros.

  Summary: Follows a prehistoric deer through his day as he searches for fresh grass to eat, seeks to avoid hungry predators, and flees from a fire.
  1. Megaceros—Juvenile literature.   2. Paleontology —Pleistocene—Juvenile literature.   [1. Megaceros. 2. Mammals, Fossil.   3. Prehistoric animals] I. Howatt, Andrew, ill. II. Title.
  QE882.U3045 1986   569'.73   86-626
  ISBN 0-86592-846-0

Rourke Enterprises, Inc.
Vero Beach, FL 32964

Megaceros

Saber Tooth Tiger

Cave Bear

Ice-Age Monsters
Megaceros

Woolly Rhinoceros

Mastodon

Glyptodon

Megaceros lowered his head and charged again. This time his antlers struck hard into those of the other giant deer and held firm. Before, his huge spread of antlers had slipped loose after the initial crashing contact. Using all his strength, Megaceros pushed against the other deer and twisted his head sideways. If he could just push the other deer off balance he would win the fight.

However, Megaceros lost his footing and stumbled backward as his opponent thrust hard. Megaceros realized that he was not strong enough to defeat the other deer. With a cry of submission, Megaceros disengaged his antlers and backed away.

Megaceros took one last look at the female deer over which he and the stronger stag had been fighting. Then, he crept away down the hillside. Perhaps there would be other females elsewhere. At the bottom of the slope Megaceros stopped to graze. The grass was not very tasty. It was dry and brittle and Megaceros did not like it. He looked to see if there was any greener grass nearby, but all around the grass was brown and dry. It had not rained for many days and the sun had withered the vegetation.

Nearby, a group of Woolly Rhinoceroses were grazing. Perhaps they had found a patch of green grass. Megaceros trotted over to check, but the grass was as poor there as anywhere else. Megaceros decided to move on in the hope of finding some better grazing.

As Megaceros moved across the wide open landscape, he noticed a familiar smell. He stopped in alarm and looked around. Megaceros had smelled the scent of wolves and he knew that wolves were dangerous. Nearby, a group of reindeer were grazing on the thin grass. They did not seem to have smelled the wolves. Megaceros saw the dangerous hunters. They were sneaking up on the reindeer.

Suddenly, the wolves leaped from cover and ran toward the reindeer. The deer scattered and began to run as fast as they could. One of them seemed to have a stiff leg. The wolves singled out this slower reindeer and chased it as fast as they could. Soon, the chase was over and the hungry hunters were stripping the flesh from it.

The wolves appeared to be busy eating the reindeer which they had killed, but Megaceros knew that they could still be dangerous. Quickly, he moved away from the scene of the hunt. Not too far away Megaceros could see a strip of green. Thinking it was fresh grass, Megaceros ran eagerly toward it.

When Megaceros reached the green grass he began to eat contentedly. The grass here was juicy and succulent. He was soon joined by some Musk Oxen. Megaceros had not realized just how hungry he was until he started eating. Now that he had found some tasty food, he ate and ate.

One of the Musk Oxen stamped its foot and made a strange sound. Suddenly, the Musk Oxen ran together in a group and stood still. They formed a ring with their huge, shaggy heads facing outward and with their dangerous horns lowered. Megaceros knew at once that something was wrong. Musk Oxen only behaved like this if danger threatened them and danger usually meant a large meat eating hunter.

Megaceros looked around to see if he could spot the danger. He did not have to look very far. A Homotherium was running across the landscape nearby. Megaceros knew Homotherium to be a large and dangerous hunter, but this one did not seem to be threatening. Around the feet of the Homotherium a pair of cubs were running about playfully. The Homotherium had just eaten a large meal and was more concerned with her cubs than with hunting.

As the Homotherium ambled out of sight the Musk Oxen scattered and started to graze again. Megaceros felt the ground with his feet. It was soft and muddy. This puzzled Megaceros, for all around was the hard baked ground where the sun had dried up all the moisture. Then, Megaceros smelled water. He moved in the direction from which the scent seemed to be coming.

Snaking its way across the grasslands was a broad, shallow stream. It was this stream which was providing the water for the green grass which grew along its banks. Megaceros splashed into the stream to drink.

Having drunk his fill, Megaceros splashed out of the stream on the far side. He shook himself to dry off and then began to graze on the rich grass. Megaceros moved from one particularly tasty clump of grass to another. His grazing took Megaceros slowly further and further away from the stream. After a while he came quite close to a group of Woolly Mammoths. In a hollow near the trees, Megaceros found some green grass, though all around was the sunbaked plain.

Then, a strange scent came to Megaceros. It was familiar, but Megaceros could not remember where he had smelled it before nor what it meant. It was not the scent of any predator he could recognize. Some distance away a cloud of smoke rose up from the dry grass. Megaceros recognized the strange smell now. It was fire.

Fire was far more dangerous than any hunter Megaceros had ever met. His great antlers would be no defense against the smoke and flames. His only chance was to run. Megaceros began to run from the flames and toward the stream. The grass was dry and the flames leaped along quickly. Megaceros was very frightened and ran blindly in a panic. He had to escape the flames.

Megaceros had almost reached the stream when a man appeared from among the rushes. Frightened as Megaceros was, he could still recognize danger. As the man thrust at Megaceros with his spear the deer dodged to one side and leaped into the waters of the stream. The man did not chase him but attacked a Woolly Mammoth instead.

As Megaceros splashed out of the far side of the stream he looked behind him. The fire was dying as it reached the damp grass by the stream and Megaceros knew that the danger from the fire was over. The man who had been lying in wait by the stream had plunged his spear into a Woolly Mammoth. He was joined by other men who also had spears and together they killed the Woolly Mammoth.

Megaceros walked away from the group of men, for he knew them to be the most dangerous hunters of all. Over a hill and out of sight of the men loped Megaceros, heading for the safety of a clump of trees. There, for the time being, he would be safe.

Megaceros and Ice Age Europe

The Ice Age

Today the sea around the North Pole and the land around the South Pole are covered by vast sheets of solid ice many hundreds of feet thick. These are known as the polar ice caps and have an important effect on the weather of the world. Today they cover about 10 percent of the world's surface, but several times in the past two million years the polar ice caps have spread out to cover more than three times as much land. The massive sheets of ice crept out to reach as far as the Great Lakes in North America and well into central Europe and Asia. This had a tremendous effect on the climates of the world. Great changes were experienced all over the world. The equator became largely desert-like, while the bands of temperate forestland and tundra were shifted much further south. Tundra is the name given to the type of landscape found near to the polar ice caps. It is generally open land which has short Summers and long, cold Winters. The Winters are so severe that large plants, such as trees, cannot survive and only stunted trees and bushes live. The short Summer, however, brings hot weather and grass and flowers thrive. This story is set on the tundra which spread right across Europe some 25,000 years ago. Strangely enough the periods of time in between the ice ages were even warmer than the climates of today.

Megaceros – the Irish Elk

Huge antlers, up to 14 feet across

Efficient teeth for grinding up food

Large size to conserve heat
Strong muscles for fighting each other and predators

The Giant Deer

The scientific name "Megaceros" means "Giant Deer". This is a very apt name for this creature. It was much larger than any deer alive today and considerably more powerful. It is thought that this huge size may have been an adaptation to the cold weather of the Ice Ages. Large size means that there is less surface area in proportion to bulk. Since heat is lost through the surface, a large animal finds it easier to stay warmer than a small animal. Perhaps the most noticeable feature of the Megaceros, however, was its enormous spread of antlers. In some cases the antlers measured 14ft from tip to tip. The animal probably used these huge antlers as much as modern deer use theirs. Antlers are used for wrestling with each other during the mating season and for defending themselves against hunters. The Megaceros is often known as the Irish Elk, though it was not an elk and was not found only in Ireland. Since the antlers rather resembled elk antlers people then thought it must have been a type of elk. Though scientists now know it to have been a different type of deer altogether, the name has stuck. Not all Megaceros were so large. On the islands of Malta in the Mediterranean Sea, a type developed which was only four feet tall due to the lack of food.

Some present day members of the deer family

Red deer

Muntjac

Fallow deer

Ice Age Animals

The animals which Megaceros encounters in the story were typical of the kind of animal to be found on the tundra during the Ice Ages. Many of these animals were especially adapted to a life in cold weather, but they did not all evolve into the huge size of Megaceros. The famous Woolly Mammoth was a type of elephant which managed to survive by evolving a thick coat to keep itself warm. The covering was made of two layers. There was long, coarse fur which protected the animal from wind and snow. Underneath this coat, was found softer, finer fur which was ideal for retaining heat. The Woolly Rhinoceros managed to survive by developing a very similar type of coat. The Musk Oxen were likewise covered with thick fur to defeat the cold. Musk Oxen can still be found living on the tundra today, though they are rather rare. Their habit of bunching together with their horns facing outward when threatened is a very effective defense against attack. The reindeer are also still to be found in the colder regions of the world and are still very common. In northern Scandinavia they are kept in herds by people called Lapps and are an important part of the economy. Homotherium has now died out. In fact it was the very end of the evolutionary line which had included such ferocious beasts as the Saber Tooth Tiger. This branch of the cat family had separated from the biting cats about 30 million years ago. All the cats, both large and small, which are still alive today are biting cats. The wolf, of course, is still very much with us and is an integral part of the wildlife of the world.

Man

Of all the hunters which roamed the tundra in the Ice Ages, the most important was man. Man had evolved many hundreds of thousands of years earlier and during the Ice Ages his technology reached the point where he could have an important effect on the world around him. Mankind had discovered the use of fire and was constantly developing new and more effective weapons with which to hunt. This meant that he was capable of tackling animals as large as Woolly Mammoths without too much difficulty. At the same time his population was expanding to unprecedented levels. It has even been suggested that man caused the extinction of many Ice Age animals. It is certain that once the ice sheets had retreated, man would soon tame the landscape to produce the world we know today.